COME, CLIMB TOWARD
GOD:
ARE YOU HUNGRY FOR
GOD?

M ARIANNA A LBRITTON

Contents

ACKNOWLEDGMENTS

Surely no one writes a book alone. Many thanks to Garnet Eubanks who helped me in this new endeavor more ways than can be counted. Thanks to my Sunday School Classes over the years, and my present church, Rocky Creek, Lucedale, MS. Also thank you to all the women who came up to me after Bible Studies who said to me "you ought to write a book." To my sister-in-law Janice Welborn, Sally Jo Ezell, Linda Cooley, and other people who kept reminding me and giving me a push now and then, well I finally wrote a book with a lot of assistance from God. I do not want to leave out anyone's name that helped me so I say Thank you, Thank you to everyone.

It would not be right to leave out all the men who prayed, and asked about progress and encouraged me. Thanks to the men who came to my Sunday Night Classes and special subject classes. To my Pastor, Greg Barker, and others I would like to say your support has meant a lot to me. To my husband, Allen, who had to endure late meals, dirty dishes, and full laundry hampers, thank you, that is true love. To my sons, Matt and Ben who prayed for me and checked on me to make sure I was writing on this book, I say,"You are the greatest."Thank you.

DEDICATION

I dedicate this book to Brother David and Sarah Grisham. Brother David encouraged me to use my spiritual gifts and gave me opportunities to use them in our church. Sarah pushed me to write and helped to open the doors for me to do so. I cannot thank you enough, but God can. May He richly continue to bless you in your ministries.

INTRODUCTION

"Where is the ladder? I cannot reach the apples." I saw a beautiful yellow apple with a red blush on an apple tree in Allen's orchard. Its' beauty made me want that one, but I could not reach it. As it is with most things of greater height than I am, I needed a step stool or a ladder. My husband brought a ladder and soon I had the apple I wanted. Several things need to be considered when you start to use a ladder. Make sure the ladder is tall enough to reach the height you need, make sure it is placed on a firm foundation and make sure the ladder is strong enough to hold you. As you begin to think of an imaginary ladder as a facilitator of spiritual growth in satisfying unidentified hunger, you can be sure that the foundation the ladder leans against are strong enough to hold you, is long enough to reach Heaven, and it is on a firm foundation.

All that week I was thinking about what God wanted me to teach at the next monthly Bible Study Group. Growing in spiritual development was on my mind, but I was not sure how to develop the lesson. Wanting that apple gave me the insight on the framework for the study. Maybe climbing a ladder would be a good illustration of the hunger pangs leading to deeper growth in Jesus involves. As you grow spiritually, understanding how the members of the Triunity work together as the One God becomes closer to you.

Growing into a mature Christian is God's desire for believers. To satisfy unknown hunger is like climbing a ladder of which the rungs are obscured by clouds. Walking by faith, one step at a time, climbing one rung of the ladder at a time is God's way to lead a believer into a deeper relationship with Him. Spiritual growth is not about **religion,** but rather a **relationship** with God. This process is like meeting a new person and gradually developing a friendship by spending time getting to know that person.

Walking by faith is a lot like walking in clouds. I can't see where I am going, but I trust the one I am following, Jesus. Just as there are stages of growth after a person is born such as infancy, toddler, child, teen, young adult, adult, and older adult, so there are stages of growth in the believer's life. The difference in physical growth and spiritual growth is *a choice*. Do you have an unexplainable hunger? Will you go to God to find out what spiritual hunger means? Such hunger can only be filled by God.

CHAPTER 1

SEEKING JESUS

I would like to share with you some of my experiences in developing a relationship with Jesus. He is the only way to satisfy deep hunger in the soul. This process results in spiritual growth with a growing deeper relationship. There were times I thought I could not answer the call to follow Jesus into the unknown, but the wonderful grace of God kept calling me forward. This is not about being a "super Christian". It is about being a "growing Christian". It is about making a choice to meet God, serve Him, and know in the depths of your being that Jesus is a real person. He likes nothing as much as having fellowship with you. My desire and prayer for you as you read and study this book is that you will be able to understand the calls of God in your life and that you will find the answer to unknown hunger in your soul. I pray you will have a relationship with Him, not just know about Him as an historical person nor only know Him as the One who will keep you out of Hell. Every Christian's walk with God is individually designed by Him.

The calling points toward spiritual growth may be in a different order than mine, but the calling points will be similar. Calling and growing points are determined by your spiritual gifts, and your personality. So, look forward with joy and anticipation to a great adventure with Jesus. Every call you answer "yes" will lead you to a good and enjoyable place in your continued fellowship with God. This book does not cover all the steps a Christian may take in a growing relationship toward getting to know God as a person. However, these are the first major steps to growth.

The first ***calling point is seeking Jesus*** to fill the unknown hunger pricking your soul. The Bible says the one who seeks finds and the one who asks receives (Matthew 7: 7&8) When a person hungers for God, the Holy Spirit pulls that one toward Jesus. The sense of something missing in life begins to occupy one's thoughts. The Holy Spirit emphasizes the hunger for God. This hunger brings a spiritual call into a person's life.

For the first time, a person begins to think about God in a personal way. Questions begin to arise in one's mind about "how to find God, how to belong to God, or what does God want me to do". This hunger is placed in a person by the Holy Spirit. The Holy Spirit puts hunger for God in each person's soul and spirit at some time in one's life. (John: 6:44a)

The response a person makes to this call of God by the Holy Spirit determines one's eternal destiny. God never forces anyone to come to Him. This call is individually made. It must be individually answered. God never forces a person to move beyond a comfort level; He will encourage. If there is a sense of force, it is coming from some source other than God.

Some people have a problem with the simplicity of meeting and responding to God. Salvation is received by believing in Jesus as the Son of God who paid everything required for redemption. To understand what is needed for our individual redemption, we need to go back to the book of Genesis and the laws of the Old Testament to realize the impact of, and responsibility of individual sin. Then one must come to realize it would take a perfect man to be able to meet the qualifications to be the perfect payment on our behalf. (Hebrews 9: 22 & 28a). Certain people have said to me, "surely salvation can't be that easy." Yes, being saved is that easy. However, it was not easy for Jesus to pay the price. Only belief in Jesus is needed to be saved. Because belief is like a coin, you can understand one side is faith and the other is repentance. Since Jesus paid the price of redemption by shedding His blood on the cross and rising from death, any person can be saved by asking Jesus to come into one's life. Repentance means to make a choice to turn one's direction in life, and decide to go God's direction. The wonderful grace of God makes this and all other Heavenly blessings possible.

I remember an amazing example of how the Holy Spirit moves a person into position to be saved if hunger for God is in a person's soul. The Ladies' Bible Study Group at Big Level Church asked me to teach a weekend retreat. Ladies from Shady Grove Church, Lucedale, MS, came and my sister-in-law brought some ladies from her church in Laurel. One day before the retreat, a friend from Shady Grove Church called me and asked if she could bring a friend of hers. She said, "Will it be alright if she is a different race?" I replied that it did not matter she would be welcome. Since that request was out of the ordinary, I became excited because that sounded like God was up to something good.

As the ladies arrived, introductions were made, food of all kinds were set up on a table, and soon laughter filled the classroom. Listening to the camaraderie caused me to remember the verse about where God is there is joy. (Psalm16:11) I was waiting for Judy and Lee to come. I believed the Holy Spirit had prepared the ladies to be accepting of Lee. When she arrived, we found her to be a delightful person whom we felt we had always known. God does all things well. As we proceeded with the study and different ladies asked questions or contributed a thought, the part about how to be saved came up in the discussion. Lee asked," How does a person get saved?" That was a surprise for me in the middle of a study. But God gave me the composure to explain the plan of salvation. I just knew that the other ladies were praying for Lee as I talked. She was saved right then. Well, that broke up the study while we all rejoiced for a while. (I was teaching the Bible Study that inspired this book.) Isn't God just amazing? Only He could bring everything together so perfectly. God's thoughts are so far above human thinking that He had to give people a simple plan to find Him. To express belief in Jesus, follow the three "A's":

1.) **ASK** Jesus to save you from sin.

2.) **ACKNOWLEDGE** Jesus died on the cross to pay all debts for you for all time.

3.) **ADMIT** Jesus kept His Word and saved you.

Do not expect some sign, nor some sound. Faith must be first. Faith is a fact. Faith is not about feeling, nor sight. However, in the days to come, you will notice a peace you never knew before, joy may bubble up when least expected, and the sense of condemnation will go away.

You will want to be with God through His Word. Please do not start your reading and studying with the book of Revelation. Many new believers are so fascinated with this book they get lost and stop studying the Bible because the symbolism and happenings become overwhelming. Your hunger and growth in fellowship with Jesus will be well developed if you will begin in the Gospel of John who writes about Jesus' divinity and humanity. Get to know Him as fully God and fully man.

Then you will benefit from studying the book of Mark and of all the Gospels. Add the study of Paul's writings next by beginning with the book of Romans. Remember: your salvation is based on Jesus' paying the price which is a permanent payment. Since redemption required the perfect and flawless blood of Jesus, then there is not one thing a a human being could add that could contribute to a person's standing with God.

CHAPTER 2

LORDSHIP

The next calling point is **Lordship**. Over the years of my own experiences, the experiences of the people in my Bible Studies, and in individual discussions, I have found some people have a real problem with this calling. I think the reason this happens is the lack of knowledge concerning the calls of God after the salvation experience. Preachers, Teachers, and Witnesses often ask if a person wants to accept Jesus as Lord and Savior. Jesus is both Lord and Savior. He is Savior first, then the calling for Lordship comes next. A problem arises concerning the age of the inquiring person. A young child can understand the call to salvation, and so too can an older person. The problem is: can the young person possibly understand what the Lordship of Jesus means? I do not think so. For a person who is saved at a young age, the Lordship calling may not come until an older age of teen or young adulthood. A young child can be saved, but cannot possibly understand Lordship. Lordship does not come into full bloom until a person comes to an understanding of what the Lordship of Jesus means. For the young, Jesus usually calls in His ownership papers when a person is in the twenty's age group.

For a person who is saved at an older age, Lordship and Salvation may be understood and acted upon immediately. I was saved when I was twelve years old. I understood asking Jesus to save me. I had no idea what Lordship meant. I think a lot of other people may be or have been in the same place. When I was 20 years old, the calling of God came much like the call to salvation. I was very confused. There was no one who seemed to know or understand what I was experiencing.

I have seen this struggle in many people over the years in the churches in which we have joined and worked. A person is being called to Lordship but does not know what the feeling of conviction means. So, the person thinks "maybe I'm not saved" and goes to the pastor or revival preacher for counseling only to be re-baptized. After a few days pass, the person finds the same pulling of the Holy Spirit. Then the person is even more confused. Why isn't peace in their spirit instead of confusion and conviction? God cannot reward unbelief. He wants a person to say "yes" to Him even if the reason for yes is not fully understood. Say "yes" to God and He will show you how to follow Him in Lordship. He will make sure you find the right way. Believe in God's work in your life. Do not be influenced by people who try to make receiving salvation difficult.

In the church at the time I was growing up, we were taught that there were only two calls of God. The only calls were to salvation and the call to preach the Gospel. Here was the problem; I am female therefore the only call I could receive was to salvation. I knew I was saved when I asked Jesus to save me. God cannot lie. The Bible cannot lie. The witness of the Holy Spirit cannot lie. And this church does not believe God calls a female to preach. So where does that leave me with this pulling from God? I began to search the Scriptures, pray earnestly, and I learned that I could not be lost because God cannot lie so something else had to be happening. The Bible says anyone who asks Jesus for salvation receives salvation. (Romans 10:13)

This is when I learned about the call to Lordship. Salvation is receiving; Lordship is submitting. Salvation is a **call**; Lordship is a **crisis**. Lordship means the One who owns me and oversees me is calling in His ownership papers. "Would I be content to stay where I was? Did I want to 'get off the fence' and really be His person? Did I want to know Him as a real person and progress in a relationship with Him?" I may hesitate to answer a call to follow Jesus into the unknown right away, but when all is said and done, I cannot say "NO" to God. He loves me too much. Fear hinders people at this point to answer a new call to follow Jesus into the cloud of unknown. Human beings seem to have a first impression God would ask them to do something they do not like or go to a place they would not like to go. That thought comes from not knowing your Abba Father very well. God always wants the best for us and will satisfy our hunger with good things (Jeremiah 29:11). (Abba in Hebrew means "Daddy.")

Now the time it takes me to answer "yes" gets shorter and shorter, because I have learned He can be trusted to act for my good and His glory. Grace is so reassuring. For salvation, for surrendering to His Lordship, to answer all the calls of God, it is all about believing and receiving grace. Grace means the unlooked for and the unexpected favor of God. Three of God's men in the New Testament show the difference in the call to salvation and to Lordship. Peter's and John Mark's experiences reveal that while Jesus had saved them, these two men had not surrendered to His Lordship until some time had passed in their lives. On the other side, Saul (Paul) is an example of an older person whose salvation experience activated the Lordship of Christ in his life at the same time. I know people who were saved as adults who go right into Lordship immediately. This hunger and its satisfaction comes under God's timetable, not ours. All the calls of God expressed by hunger for Him come according to His timing.

CHAPTER 3

SERVICE

The next hunger expressed as calling is a happy, delightful advance in getting to know Jesus. This calling is to **Service.** The Holy Spirit begins to put a desire in your heart to want to serve God. You will find yourself asking," What is God's will for me?" What does He want me to do?" Believe me; God will guide you in finding just the right place to serve. You will find when He guides you to the place He is leading; the place of service will be absolutely pleasing to you. This may take a few experiments in various kinds of ministries your church have to offer. Do not give up and think you do not have a spiritual gift with which to serve. Finding your place of service is usually discovered by trial and error. (Actually, this is probably His way to let you know what is not for you.) Early attempts by nominating committees in my church tried to find a place of service for me and appointed me to be the Department Sunday School Secretary. I do not like working with numbers so after my term was over, I did not take that assignment again.

The Church Nursery Committee said they needed help. Very soon we all knew that was not for me. The more the babies cried, the more they scratched my face and neck and the redder I got.

The redder I got the more upset the babies got. I am probably the only person to be fired from the church nursery. Polly came in, saw what a fix I was in and said, "out." The committee did not ask me to serve in the nursery again.

Playing the piano was like a foreign language I could not comprehend. I could not sing. Things looked rather bad for me in the Gifts department. There is one thing I could do. I could (and can) talk. Asking so many questions and talking, talking got me sent somewhere else when an adult got weary of answering endless questions only to have me respond "why" when I was a child.

One Sunday morning when I had finished High School, and began attending Junior College, the Sunday School Superintendent came to me and said they needed someone to teach the Junior High Sunday School Class that morning. I always broke out in red blotches when I had to stand before a class to recite or read. The very thought made me nervous. After telling God I did not know what in the world He meant in asking me to teach a Sunday School Class, I prayed my SOS prayer, "LORD help!" Then I went in to teach the class. I loved teaching the class! I could even answer their questions. At last, my Spiritual Gift made its appearance. The next church year that class was mine to teach. Over fifty years I have been teaching Sunday School Classes and Bible Studies Classes. We have moved three times during our marriage because my husband's jobs changed. After finding the church we believed God wanted us to join, it would not be over three months until that church asked me to teach a class.

God knows you and the hidden abilities He gave you. Pleasure floods the soul when a believer finds a place of service. Several years later when my husband's new job moved us to Wiggins,

MS, we joined Big Level Church. Brother Allan Moseley was pastor. In one of his sermons, he said, "Do not concentrate on what you cannot do. Concentrate on what you can do." That one thought began a change in my service as I concentrated on teaching the Bible instead of fretting about not being musical, not being a good nursery worker, and not enjoying secretarial work in the church. Accepting God's plan for your life frees you from spending time on service areas that belong to some other believer. Endeavor with all your might to concentrate on serving the Lord Jesus Christ in the Spiritual Gift He gave you. Sometimes people will not understand why you will not volunteer for some position the church needs, keep your eyes and focus on what He has called you to do. And by the way, service and living the Christian Life is not about doing, but rather about being. Be in prayer and fellowship with Jesus and opportunities to serve will just about land on your doorstep.

❋

CHAPTER 4

THE CRUCIFIXION
OF THE SELF

After a time of serving, and studying the Bible, you will sense this hunger; "Is this all there is?" This hunger is the next call; *The crucifixion of the self*. Oh, how difficult this is! Self is the "I" that exerts the right to rule "me." For the most beneficial service to God and for complete trust in God for and about everything in your life, the crucifixion of self is necessary.

Crucifixion is the work of someone or something in one's life. Crucifixion cannot be self-inflicted. This call is brought about by the actions of other people or difficult circumstances directed toward you. Circumstances that are beyond your control may enter your life. All these actions are to prune out whatever keeps you from fully following Jesus. As you seek God's face to be in control of these occurrences, some part of the claim to rule yourself dies. Do not fear that you will lose a loved one or a major calamity will ruin you. You are expressing your trust in God during this process. Remember always that God is a good Father. God does not do mean nor cruel things to his beloved children. Personally, I get tired of those who blame God for sadness and misfortunes. My experience at this step was God removing what I thought was good only to be replaced with the best. I call this process "pulling the weeds" out of my life. This process can be uncomfortable.

One day, I was reading a book by A.W. Tozer, he stated the the absolute way to look at the crucifixion to self is as it relates to an actual crucifixion. In his book *Gems from Tozer*, he mentioned three facts about a crucified person. The person being crucified is not going back to his old life, the person is looking in only one direction, and the person does not have any plans of his own for the future. This is what it means to be crucified to self. Because I gave God my life in salvation and Lordship, I am not going back to life without God in control. Learning to look toward God in everything sure does cut down on mistakes. Letting God make my plans are exciting and relieves me of trying to decide what to do or where to go. From experience I can tell you, you will be very pleased after you adjust to the new in your life. Living with God in charge is GREAT.

CHAPTER 5

RESURRECTION

The next call or work of God in your life is **resurrection**. Just as Jesus was crucified, He was resurrected to new life. Jesus could do things in the resurrection that He could not do in his natural life. The pattern continues in your resurrection life. You will find you will be called to serve in ways you never thought possible. You will have opportunities to witness and not be full of fear. Look for an increase in activity pertaining to your Spiritual Gifts. An exciting aspect is a growth in the introduction of additional gifts which will enhance your ability to serve.

The ladies in Big Level Church asked me to teach a weekly Bible Study. I thought, "This is a stretch." So, each week my prayer focus would be," Lord what subject do You want me to teach this week?" At some time in that week, The Holy Spirit would give me the subject and so the studying began. Every week one or more of the ladies who came would share with me how that study was sent for them. God is so good. His great love and attitude of giving exactly what we need are sometimes just overwhelming. Do not you just love Him! During this growth time increased power in prayer and intercession for people will come forth. You probably will not notice, but other people will.

One Friday during lunch our youth minister/song leader was discussing a layperson's revival with a Pastor friend, Brother Herring. Brother Herring told Brother Martin he found plenty of men who had lay ministries who could come speak, but he could not find a woman who had a lay ministry he could ask to speak. Brother Martin opened his mouth and said, "I know one." That night I got a phone call from Brother Herring asking me to speak to Handsboro Church about how God was using my gift of teaching. I took a deep breath and said yes. (Here comes that stretch again.) Not only did I speak during that layperson's revival but that led to my going to that church to hold three-weekend women's Bible Studies. It was a real blessing, but oh my, what a stretch. Brother Martin ran from me on Sunday because he did not know what I was going to do to get him for opening his mouth. (Singing the Star-Spangled Banner at the next football game might have been even.) Seriously, I really like to teach the Bible and/or related subjects. And, I did thank him for the recommendation.

Writing Sunday School Lessons never entered my mind. After Bible Study Thursday morning, Sarah said, "Other people ought to have a chance to hear what you know." I accepted that as a compliment and did not think any more about it. In a few weeks I got a letter from the Sunday School Board asking if I would be interested in writing lessons. Talk about a stretch! The Editor of Adult Lessons sent a sample lesson for me to write. I wrote it and then got a letter asking me to write for a month, then later for three months. To my enormous surprise, people wrote me to tell me how the lessons blessed them. God's goodness was showing through again. What a blessing the whole experience was! Only God can take a "nobody" and have her do what a "somebody" usually does. If I could look into Heaven, I think Jesus would have a mischievous smile on His face. See how much fun it is to go after God and have your hunger satisfied at all levels? These are not all the calls. By now you know the hunger pangs for God means something good is coming. All you must do is cooperate.

Chapter 6

The Call to Rest

Have you noticed you are almost to the point of burnout? That is the indication of the next call God issues. This call is the ***call to rest.*** Have you ever noticed, in reading the Bible, the emphasis Jesus places on rest, and not labor? As far as I know, the only emphasis on labor mentioned is in Hebrews, where the commandment to labor is that a person labors to enter rest (Hebrews 4:11). Jesus' rest is not from activity but rest in the activity. This is learning to let go and let Jesus be responsible for the services and the results.

Rest in Jesus is calmness, the tranquility of spirit, and confidence in the promises and provision of God. One does not have to sit down and come up with some plan to serve God. In fact, at this point, I learned how frustrating and useless my own plans of service can be. A sincere Christian wants to serve the **LORD**. What I had to learn was that God will create avenues and opportunities to serve as He chooses. Did I really think God would allow a willing servant to go without service? Services not done in the atmosphere of rest are bound to fail. I came up with a sincere plan. The women in Wiggins who worked in town could have an opportunity one day a week to meet during their lunchtime for a time of prayer for special needs. My friend, Marteal, and I finally located a place in town to hold the prayer meeting. (You would not believe how difficult that was.) So, on Thursday mornings, from 11:00-1:00, we loaded the car with coffee, hot chocolate mix, and every kind of tea for a pleasurable experience while women ate their lunch and gave prayer requests.

It sounds like a good idea, doesn't it? Marteal and I went every Thursday morning at the set time for about three months. No one came. A few times one person came. Evidently, this was my idea and not God's. The effort failed. If God wants a certain ministry, He will work out all the details, make it attractive to people, and bless its work. This was an effort in labor to work for God. This was not resting so that God would provide an avenue for service. A person works in rest when God makes the opportunity.

Working in rest makes all the difference. Soon after I let the attempt for a ladies' prayer meeting go, God opened an opportunity for weekly one-on-one discipleship training with a new church member, which I really enjoyed. As usual, this was another stretch, because I had never taught one person only. And of course, I never thought of doing something like that. In the early days of service, I would worry whether I said all the needed things if I left out something important, or if I could have done more. I know now that was labor in serving. Rest trusts the Holy Spirit that you said all the needed things, spoke what was needed, and rest believes God will not let His Word return void (Isaiah 55:11).

CHAPTER 7

ABIDING IN CHRIST

The next hunger growth pang is *abiding in Christ.* This step in growth requires learning how to exercise faith in a new depth. To abide is to complete or to finish. Abide also means to stay. Here we learn to stay in Christ and not fear what we are doing, or where we are going. John says the vine is Christ; the caretaker of the vine is God, and that leaves the life force flowing through the vine to be the Holy Spirit. All power, leadership, and service are directed by the Holy Spirit because I am staying attached to Jesus. No one can be closer to God than this.

Consider the grapevine. It is planted, pruned at the proper time; bears fruit in its season, and grows. That is the way we are. There are seasons when we plant; seasons when we are pruned (which might be temporarily painful); seasons when we bear fruit (which are the happiest time), and we keep growing. In summary, think about the three aspects of salvation: *salvation, sanctification,* and *glorification.* This means a constant progression into the likeness of our Savior if we answer "Yes" and stay attached to Him. This process keeps on going until one day our **LORD** calls us to Heaven either through the death of the body or by the sound of a trumpet. Praise God. Life with Him really does get better and better. Fear not: **SHINE!**

ADDITIONAL SCRIPTURE REFERENCES

CHAPTER 1:
Seeking Jesus John 1: 12-13; John 3: 16-17;
Romans 10:9-13

CHAPTER 2:
Lordship Luke 22:32; John 20:28

CHAPTER 3:
Service
1Corinthians 12:4, 11, 28

CHAPTER 4:
The crucifixion of self Galatians 2:20;
Galatians 5: 24-25;
Galatians 6:13-15;
Colossians 2:13-15;
Ephesians 2:15-16

CHAPTER 5
Resurrection Job 42:10b-13;
Matthew 28:5-6

Study Guide

---

1. Which Scripture or Scriptures verses are your anchor verses for security in your relationship with God?
2. Do you have a believing friend with whom you can share experiences and share prayer requests"
3. Where are you on the "ladder toward God'?
4. Write about one of your learning experiences in climbing your ladder toward God.
5. What "good thing in 'doing' have you exchanged for the "best thing"?
6. Which call from God has been the most evident and therefore, easiest to say "yes"?
7. Which call from God has been the most difficult to comprehend and therefore the hardest to respond with a "yes"?
8. Isn't it wonderful to "shine" for Jesus? Write about an example of shining for Jesus that gave you a special sense of pleasure.

www.ingramcontent.com/pod-product-compliance
Lightning Source LLC
Chambersburg PA
CBHW020348130626
46549CB00003B/1352